WILDCATS

Bobcats

by Jennifer L. Marks

Consulting Editor: Gail Saunders-Smith, PhD

Consultant: Robin Keith
Senior Research Coordinator
San Diego Zoo's Institute for Conservation Research

CAPSTONE PRESS
a capstone imprint

Pebble Plus is published by Capstone Press,
151 Good Counsel Drive, P.O. Box 669, Mankato, Minnesota 56002.
www.capstonepub.com

 Books published by Capstone Press are manufactured with paper
containing at least 10 percent post-consumer waste.

Library of Congress Cataloging-in-Publication Data
Marks, Jennifer, 1979–
    Bobcats / by Jennifer L. Marks.
    p. cm.—(Pebble plus. Wildcats)
    Includes bibliographical references and index.
    Summary: "Simple text and full-color photos explain the habitat, life cycle, range, and behavior of bobcats"—
Provided by publisher.
    ISBN 978-1-4296-4480-8 (library binding)
    1. Bobcat—Juvenile literature. I. Title. II. Series.
QL737.C23M274 2011
599.75'36—dc22   2010002795

Editorial Credits
Katy Kudela, editor; Bobbie Nuytten, designer; Svetlana Zhurkin, media researcher; Eric Manske, production specialist

Photo Credits
Alamy/Kenebec Images/Val Duncan, 12–13; Papilio, 16–17
Corbis/Joe McDonald, 15
Getty Images/Altrendo Nature, 21
Minden Pictures/Matthias Breiter, 5
Photolibrary/Superstock, 19
Shutterstock/Art McKenzie, 7; Dennis Donohue, cover, back cover; Fenton (paw prints), cover and throughout;
    Chris Lorenz, 1, 11; Tom Tietz, 9

The author dedicates this book to her sister, Lisa, who adores bobcat kittens.

Note to Parents and Teachers

The Wildcats series supports national science standards related to life science. This book
describes and illustrates bobcats. The images support early readers in understanding the text.
The repetition of words and phrases helps early readers learn new words. This book also
introduces early readers to subject-specific vocabulary words, which are defined in the
Glossary section. Early readers may need assistance to read some words and to use the Table
of Contents, Glossary, Read More, Internet Sites, and Index sections of the book.

Printed in the United States of America in North Mankato, Minnesota.
032011   006102R

Table of Contents

Silent and Spotted

A bobcat quietly crosses

its snowy forest range.

The cat's ears tune in

to every sound.

Bobcats prowl through
Canada, Mexico, and
the United States.
They live in forests,
fields, and swamps.

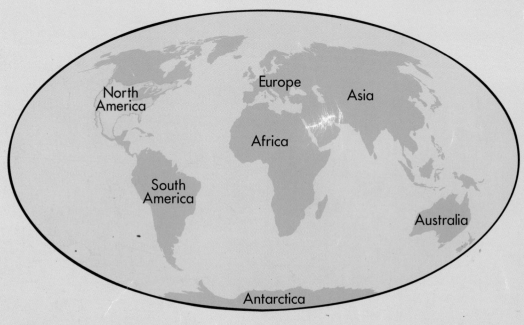

North
America

Europe

Asia

Africa

South
America

Australia

Antarctica

☐ where bobcats live

Bobcat Bodies

Bobcats are smaller than most wildcats. Adults weigh between 16 and 30 pounds (7 and 14 kilograms).

house cat

bobcat

Bobcats are named for

their short, or bobbed, tails.

Thick spotted fur

helps them blend into

their surroundings.

Patient Predators

A hunting bobcat hides.

Its yellow eyes see well,

even in dim light.

When prey is near,

the bobcat pounces.

A bobcat uses its big paws

and sharp claws

to pin down its prey.

Rabbits, deer, and rodents

are the cat's main meals.

Bobcat Life Cycle

Females have litters
of one to six kittens.
Kittens are born helpless.
They need their mothers
for food and safety.

As bobcat kittens grow,

they learn to use

their claws and teeth.

Bobcat mothers teach

their kittens how to hunt.

Around age 1, young cats

find their own territories.

They learn to live alone.

Bobcats live up to

12 years in the wild.

Glossary

dim—somewhat dark

litter—a group of animals born at the same time to one mother

pin—to hold something or someone firmly in place

pounce—to jump on something suddenly and grab it

prey—an animal hunted by another animal for food

prowl—to move around quietly and secretly

range—an area where an animal naturally lives

rodent—a mammal with large, sharp front teeth

territory—an area of land that is occupied and defended by an animal or group of animals

tune—to focus and listen carefully

Read More

Pitts, Zachary. *The Pebble First Guide to Wildcats.* Pebble First Guides. Mankato, Minn.: Capstone Press, 2009.

Riley, Joelle. *Pouncing Bobcats.* Pull Ahead Books. Minneapolis: Lerner Publications Co., 2003.

Internet Sites

FactHound offers a safe, fun way to find Internet sites related to this book. All of the sites on FactHound have been researched by our staff.

Here's all you do:

Visit *www.facthound.com*

FactHound will fetch the best sites for you!

Index

Word Count: 173
Grade: 1
Early-Intervention Level: 18